MAY THE BLESSINGS FLOW

- A Collection of Spiritually Inspiring Poems -

LEMUEL WHITELOCK

STERLING PUBLISHING GROUP

May The Blessings Flow
– A Collection of Spiritually Inspiring Poems by Lemuel Whitelock

Published by The Sterling Publishing Group, USA 1.888.689.1130
www.SterlingPublishingGroup.com

Printed in the United States of America
ISBN: 978-0-9845010-9-0

Cover and book design by Jodi Nicholson www.JodiNicholson.com
Cover photography Elakala Waterfalls Pool by www.ForestWander.com
Edited by Jodi Nicholson for SPG www.SterlingPublishingGroup.com

This book may be ordered through the publisher or by contacting the author via email at awarenesscenter@yahoo.com or by visiting online at http://awarenesscentercoaching.wordpress.com

Literature & Fiction: Poetry / Inspirational and Spiritual
Education & Reference: Quotations

Dedication

To my mother Mary, who brought me into this world, and was the first person I wanted to marry.

To my sister Bette, who tormented me as a child, and later, loved me to the very depth of my soul.

To my brother-in-law Walt, who made every conversation about me, and was my living idol.

To my Auntie Gay, who simply bubbled with joy while her face revealed her delight in life.

All are now gone into the worlds beyond, and will be there to greet me, when I cross the great divide.

TABLE OF CONTENTS

May The Blessings Flow ...

ACKNOWLEDGMENTS

There are so many that could be included and deserve recognition; I hope you know who you are.

A special thanks to my wife Valerie for all of her never-ending encouragement, and for being my partner for over 30 years and counting.

To my daughter Julia, who assisted with the editing, and for providing me with books and journals.

To my son Douglas, who is my computer guru, and has made every effort to pull me out of the dark ages of technology.

To Jodi Nicholson, my publisher, for all of her professional experience and support in putting this book of poems together.

INTRODUCTION

The poetry in this book is designed to encourage the reader to think, or to go beyond thinking into the inner worlds of knowing.

My hope is that you, the reader, may receive value from reading this collection of poems. Many were written with a guiding hand of awareness greater than that of the writer.

There is a lot of emphasis on human nature, relationships, life, Divine Spirit, and the ways of love.

It may not be a coincidence that you have picked up this book of poems. After all, each of us is here to teach one another and to gain in that experience.

THE AUTHOR'S VIEW

Here is a snapshot view of my personal perspective on life, and why it is important for people to know their inner self. We are Soul, seeking to know ourselves, and the God within us. That which we claim as our spiritual truth, evolves as we evolve in consciousness and understanding. The world by design is the way it is, and each of us are like stones in a tumbler put in this world to polish one another, as we learn the ways of Love.

All of us are equal, in that we are Soul. Yet, we are unequal in consciousness, since some Souls have been around the block far longer than others. And, there are also many enlightened Souls that are here to serve God by carrying the Light and Sound, so we may see God through their eyes.

In the end, it does not matter how many lifetimes of karma it may take, we will want to serve God with every fiber of our being. For the essence of Soul is purified Love, and Soul knows no greater joy, than that found in being of service to all life.

~ Lem

MAY THE BLESSINGS FLOW

- A Collection of Spiritually Inspiring Poems -

LEMUEL WHITELOCK

STERLING PUBLISHING GROUP

A Collection Of

POEMS ...

A WRITER'S PRAYER

What purpose could my writing serve?
If Spirit flows through me
And creates the words.

Use me Spirit that I may serve
Thee with what I say.
Let it be your wisdom that flows my way.

Keep me not in Thy way.
If there is awareness I may invoke,
Let it be your truth that is noted.

There is so much that I may gain when
You light the page before my pen,
Lessons of life, delightful insights,

The deeper depths of Love.
Spirit allow me to bring life to words,
That they may touch another heart.

THOUGHTFUL CONSIDERATION

Religion, religious politics, astral projection, psychic
phenomenon, out of the body experience —
Have you considered these or maybe others?

Some years ago, I decided to follow the path of
LOVE, and to see life from the middle road while
Not being polarized to the left or to the right.

To strive to respect people's rights to choose their
Own way of life. If they are on their chosen path,
Who am I to think I know what is best?

Can one be so filled with LOVE there is no room for
A selfish thought? What we "give" life and "take" from
life, is a freedom of choice.

And, that my friend makes all the difference.

FROM PAIN TO GAIN

No pain, no gain is a widely used expression
That may be more accepted than rejected.
It is often said about building muscles or
When becoming much more skilled physically.

Maybe you have not even considered how
Big a part it plays in the spiritual realm of life.
Yet it is often mental and emotional pain that
Teach us the most about Divine Love's grace.

When the heart has suffered in some sudden way,
While reflecting upon your pain, you may see the
Hidden blessings. With that pain, comes a greater
Consciousness of God's compassionate nature.

A THOUGHT

A thought like a flower
Nurtured can last for years or hours,
Thoughts must be monitored
For one to stay balanced.

Thoughts of fear and insecurity
Are the big dream stealers;
Thoughts of regret could or should have been
Keep one from accepting what is, once again.

Thoughts of those we love
And things we can do for them,
A thought of treating a complete stranger,
As if a long lost friend.

Thoughts that bring the action
Of sharing comfort and love
Come back to the giver in multiples.

Thoughts blossom and bloom,
They even set the mood —
Is a thought worth giving away your happiness to?

A LIT CANDLE

When a lit candle
Lights the wick of others,

Then and only then,
Can it see its own true beauty.

And that beauty continues expanding
As the candle light glows into each world.

IN ALL THE WORLD

In all the worlds
One might travel to
In all the radiant colors
One might see

In all the Souls
One might meet
There is no other
Exactly like me.

Yes, I have
My own identity,
Yet I seek
What many seek.

The burning flame of God
The heart of pure love
The open vessel
The consciousness of God!

Some may have found another way,
But only through surrender and
Service has God lit the path I take.

FARM ANIMALS

Some days I think
I would rather be a farm animal.

Look at the cows in the field
They show no prejudice about their color.

You don't see them raising a hand in anger
Or, their kids in the street begging for money.

They remain contented
And live their life in each moment.

A TEACHER AMONG US

Light in his eyes,
A smile that could lift anyone's heart,
The ability to fit in, regardless of where he was.

His name is Walt.

The patience of a saint,
A life of teaching,
Stimulating students to be creative thinkers.

His name is Walt.

A husband, brother, uncle, cousin, a friend,
Able to be in the moment up to the end,
His living example hard to comprehend,
What a spiritual presence within,
His mastery of life most humbling.

His name is Walt.

THAT STRANGER

I was standing near that stranger by the river
And could hear what the wise bearded man said;
I was truly amazed by such wisdom, truth, and
Higher consciousness being expressed.

Even more wondrous was the look in his eyes,
It was indescribable, like looking into a burning fire;
I know it could be many years before I understood
Many of the things he said.

No matter, I was transformed and brought
Into the Light, by listening to those holy words
That rolled off his tongue, and went echoing
Gently into the night.

ENVY

Who can say they never fell into its trap?
Envy robs you from having a joyful heart.
Seeing your blessings there before you and
Instead of enjoying them, you dwell upon
The gifts of another with a wanting heart.

Envy is nothing less than a thief in the night,
Stealing your satisfaction out from under you.
And can leave in its place a void, an endless pit,
Of the foulest known disgruntlement. The more
You focus upon it, the more its pit consumes you.

Until you realize that others have at some level
Earned their gifts, as you have earned yours,
You remain stuck within the pit and you may not
Even see, that your dilemma is totally self-inflicted.

WITH GRIEF

All seems lost,
Nothing left to gain,
Pain numbing deep inside
You remain in the dimness,
It surrounds you, as you
Feel too weak to fight.
No wind in your sail,
Or lift in your feet,
Just drudgery
You hear a voice
Speaking softly within ...
"Your life is not finished.
It is all right to be sad.
But not to make it your life;
You can and will bounce back.
You are not betraying anyone
When you start spontaneously,
Laughing joyfully again."

BEYOND YOUR CONSCIOUSNESS

Consciousness, like truth, evolves with awareness.
So is there practical truth or consciousness without
One's awareness of it?

How can one speak of what they do not know?
Unless, they are a politician, then it is expected,
Isn't it? That's a side joke, so don't put all your
Attention on it.

You might have just laughed; I did when I wrote it.
Yet making fun of any group of people, regardless
Of how frequently we do it, still builds karma.

What you don't know can hurt you, as much as
Anything you know. Spiritual laws are not made to be
Broken.

They are the recognition of God's truth, which
Often cannot be spoken. Yet those that can tune
Their spiritual inner ear understands Its' wisdom.

BE

Those that seek, see God.

Yet, those that be, become God.

Be the God you seek.

BALANCING ACT

How easy it can be for us to miss the point.
Many of us may have even missed our boat.
Every single event or occurrence can be
A vital part of our spiritual journey.

Can we remain stable, in our spiritual vessel,
When the mind is in the red sea of anger?
Can we keep our life in balance while we
Journey between duality and the God worlds?

The chance for growth is provided by each
Of our daily encounters, without exception.
It is so important that we locate a teacher
Who has the traits we want to emulate.

Life's about a journey of opportunities,
Many of which we are openly seeking,
And many we avoid like the plague of death.
Discernment is needed to obtain our mission.

If we just keep taking baby steps,
We have plenty of time for discovery.
Our spiritual awareness is never a race;
It is the practice of seeing God, in every face.

BECOMING

Becoming what you have always been:
Soul, eternal, a spark of God, a gift,
A blessing, and a fountain of love,

A spiritual being on the physical plane,
With the most often asked question, why?
So, God put you here to learn the ways of love,

Yet, so often you may flounder, dealing with
The minute minutia, while the higher view is
Just outside your awareness or human radar.

Follow the path of love, be who you really are,
Solve the mysteries, and put your puzzle
Back into harmony with God.

BOUND

Here we stand bound in chains,
Created by the mind.

Amongst the Law of Plenty,
The mind has put us in a maze.

A maze of chambers that lead
Only to distress and death.

Yet, when we place all our love
Upon the Grace of God,

And evoke constant diligence,
Divine Love begins directing our path.

It sets us free from that
Torturous maze of a painful death,

Into the light of the Master's footprints,
Where Soul finds true peacefulness.

Knowing the Law of Plenty is
The freedom pass of consciousness.

DANCING SOUL

There is so much we do not know,
Yet, have you felt the dancing soul?
The joy within that does not end and
Yet, your mind loses it all the time.

Life is really not about what we think
Or believe, but the truth we know inside.
Enlightenment should be no surprise;
God wants you to be the dancing soul.

CONFLICTED

When do we surrender?
When do we muddle through?

What if we did this or that?
What if we didn't do this or that?

With so many considerations,
We catapult into the murky space.

With an awakened realization,
We can recognize the cloud of illusion.

What counts is being connected
With our Divine Creator's love.

Whatever's left, is Maha Kal's
Work of designed distraction.

LOSS OR GAIN

Loss or a gain …
You can gain what you lost,
You can lose what you gain,
Different sides of the same thing.

Sometimes a loss is really a gain,
Sometimes a gain is really a loss.
In the big picture, does it matter?
You decide: what does or doesn't.

FINDING YOURSELF

It is never, never too late
To make a complete fool of yourself,
While you're leaving your mind behind
And reaching out to catch the wings of God!

It requires you to be uniquely you,
Setting your sight within the spiritual realm,
Reaching for God with all your heart and soul,
While being a forever devotee of the Divine One.

Look within to find your spiritual teacher,
While always following the path of pure love.
For in the wings of God is the essence of love, with
Endless possibilities and fireworks bursting into joy.

I SIMPLY MUST

I simply must be love SUGMAD,
It is my calling and burning desire,
I have no choice, nor do I seek any,
All I know is that I must.

My purpose drives this passion within.
It is like wanting to leap into your water
As this pure waterfall cascades over a
Thousand feet to emit a thunderous roar.

And I am consumed in its overwhelming
Power and the compelling attraction of
This Divine Cosmic presence of love.
I simply must be that, Holy SUGMAD.

PRACTICAL WISDOM

The greatest minds throughout time
Have provided so much practical wisdom
And few may be more important than
Life gives you what you are expecting.

Your tendency, belief, and considerations
Have been controlling much of your life.
You may be doing everything just right,
But have a nagging fear it is not to be,
And those very thoughts bring failure.

It is not that you are unworthy, but
It is a result of your negative thoughts
Being intertwined in a belief system.

SELFLESSLY

There are many good deeds
Done for recognition, ego or pride.
The pat on the back by others or
A certain promotion ...

Often overlooked are the rewards
Selflessly obtained by selfless deeds.
The flourishing of God's Divine Love
Simply blossoms within us.

THE GREATEST GIFT

Lord how many times have I asked you
To help lighten my burdensome load

Only to cuddle my problems again
Like a mother hen with baby chicks?

I am a creature of habit;
Lord, it is not your fault.

Maybe I should have been asking
For you to help me change.

To be able to let my life flow,
Without attachment to the results,

And to be able to recognize and
Appreciate your spark in all of us.

For you created us in your image,
To bring your love to one another.

Love is the greatest gift we have and
Its only limitation is if one's heart is closed.

SPIRIT OF LOVE

In the spirit of love,
I sat down to rejoice in my blessings
As ITs gentle arms surround me.

Wanting nothing more than to be near Thee,
As a devotee of your loving ways,
And capture that essence in me that is Thee.

All the depth of my love I give Thee.
Show me the ways that I may serve;
For always, I am Thine.

THE CALL OF SOUL

A restless Soul has a driving need
To be reconnected with Divine Spirit.
At the coinciding moment that Soul
Cries out from the depth to be found,
The Sat Guru is calling for Soul!

It is no coincidence, for that reconnection
Has occurred again, and yet again, as
Soul's destiny has always been to return
To the very heart of its Creator, and to
Serve the consciousness of Divine Love.

THE EXPANDING PERSPECTIVE

It is really easy to be disappointed in others.
They don't say what you want to hear or
Forget something really important you shared.

They don't understand just how you feel.
You are not the center of their world,
Even though you think you should be.

But, life is so much more than your eyes see.
You can see better when you change focus
And look through the eyes of another.

Who's right is not as important as being a friend.
You can have so much more in your relationship;
See the world through your heart, not your pride.

THE NOW

As we experience our now,
All that is, is being painted in it.
The past influences the present
As our karma carries forward.

The future is influenced by
The thoughts you are having
At this very moment.

Yet, it is in the space of now
Where all truth is found.
And where you place your
Attention, paints the picture
Of your life.

The flow of the living colors
Are all present when following
The true calling of your choosing.

THE SAT GURU'S PROMISE

I am with you when you know it.
I am with you if your blinders are on.
I want to be invited into your heart,
So you're living a conscious choice.

I will never leave you, even when you
Feel totally withdrawn, my compassion
And protection is constantly present.
Each chela's guidance is never abandoned,

Even while in those dark nights of Soul.
Once taken upon my wings, your tutelage
As co-worker with God, has already begun.
Soul awakens into the pure worlds of Love.

THE PUREST LOVE

We are the joy of the purest love;
That is the very IS part of us.
A presence that never comes or goes;
It is our true constant self.

We find it by singing love songs to God,
In repeating those Holy names of God,
Through building this bridge to Soul,
We discover what is always here.

Each of us wants to help another;
It is our true natural nature of love.
When connected to our inner world,
We become channels of the purest love.

THE WAY IS SIMPLE

Follow God's jewels of love,
That magnetic bond of divineness,
As love always attracts more love.

The purest path is simple,
Follow your heart as it is drawn
To the very heart of creation.

Our true home

THE RIVER

I am the river that sings,
As it dances over its bed of rocks,
The sound inspiringly pure.

I am the river that sparkles with light,
As the sun plays with my surface,
Then warms my joyful spirit.

I am the river that loves,
With all its consciousness, and
Blessings are returned so many folds.

I am the river that overflows its banks,
As the tears swell up from my core,
These tears of gratitude purify my soul.

I am the river of cascades,
As the falls are fast approaching, my
Spirit sores within the endless mist.

I am the river of truth,
Not trapped by veiled illusion, those
Seeking love discover their purpose.

YOU STOOD THERE

You stood there at the door so many lifetimes,
Too shy to knock or open it.

This time, somewhere deep within, confidence
Suddenly appears and pushes the mind aside.

The door now opens before your eyes, revealing
Your reflection within the radiant face of God.

UNDERSTANDING

Do you understand; the mind
Is in the shadow of the soul?
Yet, if not controlled, it is
The mind which runs away
With thoughtless thought.

Only by exercising the
Awareness of soul, can you
Conquer the mind. It requires
A conscious connection with
The Source.

Giving the soul the Light and
Sound, and like a child it will
Skip its way to God. To the joy
Of the most devoted parent,
Now waiting with open arms,
And a blinding smile.

THE WAYS OF VIRTUE

The virtuous ways are not designed
To make the mind, or little self, happy.
The precise stepping stones of virtue
Are narrow and unexpectedly slippery.

Each step repeats in a random order,
So best stay on your toes. These steps
Include: humbleness and detachment,
Discernment and forgiveness, along
With tolerance and contentment.

If you forget what step you are on,
Be thoughtfully loving, and that will
Keep you on your way to the truest
Love of all.

YOU ARE MY FRIEND

You are a rose pedal
Floating on the holy
River HU,

And as you sing,
HU, HU, HU,
You feel the dancing

Water joyously twirling
Beneath you,
And a fullness of confidence

Seldom, if ever experienced.
Simply knowing that the love of
The HU is the ALL of ALL,

You awaken into the most
Precious of roses, in the very
Heart of the Divine HU.

A MIRACLE

Is it any less of a miracle
If we were molded from the hands of GOD,
Evolved through evolution, or arrived here
Via air transport from a distant world?

What makes us so unique is our ability
To imagine and ponder these possibilities.

And, we can strive to master Unconditional,
Divine Love. That alone, is what makes us
More like GOD.

A PERFECT MORNING

A perfect morning in Africa
Waiting for the Captain
To say, "Climb aboard".

We hop in on our sides,
And are lifted to the upright position,
Then, suddenly we are above the ground.

An experience of a lifetime
Overlooking the Serengeti
Seeing wildlife from a distance

Then, they are so close
And showing no fear
Until the propane burner is heard.

Seeing these majestic creatures
Where they belong, and being
Protected from human harm

God help us to keep it that way,
So other generations can also
Enjoy this amazing experience some day.

YOU, YOU, YOU

It is all true: your life is up to you. You can
Live in "try" or make your dreams come true.
When you are on purpose, standing in your truth,
In your higher self, answers flow through you.

Keep taking your goal steps each and every day.
For when your intentions are aligned, your goal
Steps keep you on track to your desired destination.
Taking those action steps can always conquer fear.

Everyone, needs a little help, even you from time to
Time. Work with those that have the coaching skills,
To question you about your "why". And remember
The value of humor; it is good to laugh at yourself.

When you are keeping the big picture, there in
Front of your eyes, those obstacles become your
Stepping stones as the blessings continue flowing
Into your successfully balanced life.

ANY RELATIONSHIP

Any sort of relationship
Can run rather smooth

Unless expectations poke
Out their little heads
To get a better view.

Then, if they go unchecked,
They spoil everything they touch.

And that which was
So beautiful is now
Suspect and in distress.

Stormy sea at night,
by Ivan Aivazovsky 1849

AS YOU WOULD

If you ask me have I changed?
I carry you in my spirit, in my heart,
And every fiber of my soul.

You, my dearest love, have taught
Me how to love, to cherish life,
And to grasp life with both hands.

I know the oneness that two
Loving hearts share, as
Your heart is my heart.

When in my deepest grief
And at the peak of my despair,
I see your gentle smiling face.

I know you watch over me.
It is your physical presence,
Not your spirit, I am without.

I now honor you, by striving to heal,
And find happiness and purpose,
As you would have me do.

CONDITIONAL TRADITIONAL DANCE

I want what is best for you,
But I have my needs too!

I want to make you happy,
But not at the expense of my happiness.

I want you to be completely devoted to me,
But not because I want you to be.

I want you to simply know what I am thinking,
But not if it is something you shouldn't know.

I want to be the first person you think of always,
But you must keep those thoughts loving and kind.

I want you to be exactly the way you are.
But make sure you follow all my conditions too!

AT OUR ESSENCE

Are we anything
     Other than spirit?

Could spirit be anything
     Other than love?

If we could be anything
     More than love,

     Let us be more love!!!

BROTHER

He is my brother by love, not birth.
Our friendship melted away my worries,
With his assuring words, my attitude
Simply clay in majestic hands

His body and head consumed with
Cancer, he defied it, living over a
Year beyond what the doctors said,
And even on his dying day

He declared, he was not going anywhere.
But, God knew his struggle was done
And called him back home, yet grasping
Hands hold me captive to an endless void.

BE THE LIGHT

In the sheer light of dawn,
It dances before my eyes,
This amazing Light of God.

It fills my soul with color,
With life and bright joy,
As I raise my hands for shade.

I realize the Light now
Comes from within, not out;
It is I who holds the Light.

The Light within speaks,
I AM, THAT I AM,
I now understand.

The spark of God in me,
Keeps expanding as I sing
HU, with an open heart.

ECHOES OF LOVE

In the echoes of love and loss,
The heart is broken apart,
Healing so far away in the dark

Tears flowing like rivers upon my cheeks,
Crying sounds come from the deep,
Where dear God is my loved one now?

How could it be she was called home?
I never felt so completely alone.
Couldn't I be with her once again?

Looking into her loving eyes, while
Kissing her on her sweet puffy lips, and
Holding her close enough to feel as one.

Now, I suddenly feel her here with me,
And here, within my loving vision,
We are endlessly connected by Spirit.

When I become engulfed in pain again,
I need always to be reminded that
Those bonded by the heart, shall never part.

DANCING WITH GOD

Of all the things my heart desires,
It desires to dance with God.

Being held in God's arms of grace,
Feeling the uplifting of Soul,

As it twirls in the divineness of joy,
While in the comforting bliss

Of the Almighty's constant love.

PASSION

Do a deed with passion, enthusiasm, and pleasure.
Why would you want to make life a chore?
When, just by changing your attitude, it's a blessing.

How come you struggle so long and so hard?
Don't you know you are creating your own karma?
Why face the new day in the same tired way?

You can be the one with dynamic charisma,
The one who channels pure Divine Love,
Through seeking the path of the higher self.

You are here to learn from others and
Those that rub you wrong are the best teachers
On the road to self-awareness and Divine Love.

Dance with the delight of life in your joyful child,
Be in the moment, learn to live always in the now,
With passion, enthusiasm, pleasure, and love.

HAPPINESS

To be happy one must choose it,
For it is only a decision away,
No one else can make you happy.

Only you can do that for yourself,
You can pick happiness, by letting
Go of the thoughts in the way.

Practice being happy, smile all day.
Even when things go so very wrong,
Nothing can steal your happiness,

UNLESS YOU LET IT!

NOT OUT THERE

As he stood there looking at a distant star,
Wondering if someday that radiant star
Might light his way to his future life.

A voice cried from deep inside, the light
You seek, my friend, is not out there
Somewhere, but within.

He remembered; someone spoke of an inner light
And said they like to contemplate while
Singing holy names for God.

After doing this a little while each day, a blue light
Appeared before their closed eyes and a
Sweet ringing sound in their ears.

Sometimes they may see the face of an inner guide
And ask questions and listen quietly, as
Their inward journey takes flight.

PAINTING A ROSE

My friend is painting a rose
By using watercolors of red and gold.

She is more special to me than most,
A perfectionist, who overlooks my flaws.

She strives to get things just right,
But gives others the space to be who they are.

I see her as a rose of many colors
And enjoy her honesty and delightful spirit.

Her love radiates to others in countless ways,
She motivates me to search inside for truth.

As she finds herself within the experience of spirit,
Painting a rose is being in God's creative flow.

REAWAKENING

I am cold
I am scared
I am full of fear

And you call,
"I am Here"
Recognizing me as Soul

Just like a rosebud,
Blooming-
                Consciousness…

RED MAPLE

She watched as her beautiful
Red Maple started losing her leaves.

She had hoped they could
Hold on longer this year, of all years.

As she wonders how a tree handles
Losing its offspring year after year.

She stands there in deep thought until her
Knees start to buckle, then turns to walk alone.

REFLECTIONS

Here before me is a world, in a world, in a world.
The world of the sea, the world of the shore,
And the world of the sky.

Mostly, I exist on the shore or land
Yet, my eyes are captured by the sea
The waves rippling and shimmering with light.

Topped off by a calm, soft blue, cloudless sky,
As a small flock of migrating birds are flying by,
Near the water's edge, driftwood floats to shore.

Where would I rather be?
I can think of nowhere today
Yet, I feel I am the stranger here.

How I ended up here on earth is a mystery,
Still I have lessons to learn and chores to do,
Inner worlds to explore and many dreams to fulfill.

SISTER

My sister left in a hurry,
She did not wait for the jury,
While making up her own mind
About having cosmetic surgery.

I wish she had told me, it may
Have lessened my shock,
She was killed by incompetence,
But those that saw her said,
"She was beautiful in death."

SPIRITUAL KISS

Feeling the breath of love
Left me in a state of bliss,
It is like being surrounded
In a soothing morning mist.

Now, enjoying this breath of love
Even more, knowing it can carry
Me to Heaven's door, and being in
The loving mist is like a Spiritual Kiss.

Feeling so spiritually contented, I
Share this with others; love must go
To another, it is designed that way, for
Divine Love must be constantly flowing.

THE COMFORTER

She has a calling, she feels it deep within
A calling to be a comforter, a peaceful presence
In the midst of turmoil and despair.

As the ground shakes under one's feet,
The comforter is needed even more.
Yet, some feel the comforter is too passive,

Not caring enough about the issues of the day,
Yet, the comforter understands the wind of change
And does not fight what is best to let go.

She strives to master the path of the middle road.

THE FOLLY

Looking out for number one,
The folly of it all

If I master being humble,
How much more can I serve?

How much greater depth I understand,
And break those fears of insecurity.

Those fears of not having enough
Or losing that which I have

How many times have I looked at the cup
And only seen how little there?

My shallow thinking, depriving contentment;
Why Lord does the little self-control me so?

You did not put me here to worry about such,
But to learn how to serve all life,

To be a beacon for your Love,
And a servant to your flock.

THE DOOR

I stood there at the door
Of an ancient world,
One of a distant past.

Not really known to us anymore,
Unless recalling one's past life
Spent there, somewhere.

They are bare stones now,
Where once brightly painted,
Their construction designed to last.

Using a 360 degree view,
How close are we to the person
We might have been?

THE GLASS HOUSE

I sat behind a man one day
And could not help but notice
The bushes in his ears.

I began my critical assessment,
Noting if it were me, trimming surely
Would be, the order of the day.

A week or so later, as I looked
In the bathroom mirror, I was shocked
To discover the bushes I now owned.

With my newest lesson right in view,
It is so easy to see the flaws of others,
While being so blind to my own.

How clearly I see what others do,
Without realizing they simply hold the
Mirror up for me to see myself.

THE GLASS

Taking the glass,
Holding it to my lips,
I drink,
The taste more bitter than sweet.

Much of life,
Not as I had expected,
Thinking I am evolved enough,
Yet getting caught
On the bitter side of it.

Still again,
I pick up the glass,
Determined
It shall be the sweet taste
That I experience
Most in my life.

THE CORE

There is nothing so important
Than to know your inner self,
To know the core of self, itself.

That pure essence of cosmic love,
The inner joy of joyfulness,
The undaunted dancing heart

And yet, we seem satisfied with
Our busy lives of frivolous gossip,
And captivity of our inner spirit.

Now, are we simply one of the masses?
Doomed to be no more than ordinary,
Or a uniquely created individual

Only limited by our imagination,
And by the depth of our convictions,
To the truth within us.

THE MASTER'S SHOES

I knelt down to put on the Master's shoes.
As I looked at his feet, he had traveled many miles.
His feet were weathered, with thick-skinned soles.

I felt humble and honored to serve the Master,
Assisting him in some small way, for I gain
Such wisdom from this beautiful enlightened Soul.

It is a sacred gift to serve and through service
I learn so much as doors continue to open within,
Revealing the pureness of God's Divine Purpose.

THE SECRET

The secret of life
      Is to place your window

Where you want
      To enhance the inward view.

THE SEEKER

What is life, if not unexpected moments of shock
Or rewarding treasures or failures? Each moment
Can bring changing tides with new challenges.

These are opportunities for deeper understanding.

The path of gratitude, ever evolving love,
Compassion, and pure enlightenment hold
The seeker's truth; and are you not the seeker?

THE STORM

The storm blows through life many times
Sometimes, like a wise tree, we bend with the wind,
Other times, we let it pass through us.

Then, there are times we resist with all our might,
Taking a stand, refusing to give in and the hell
With the cost, relationship or job, so what?

Sometimes slowly and sometimes very fast,
We catch on to the fact, it is better to relax.
What is gained by sticking to our point of view?

Is it simply our pride we must protect at all cost?
Why not consider the other's point of view?
It's amazing what we learn when we don't want to.

There are still many times we resist with our all,
Knowing it will never make us a better man.
Yet being centered through contemplation can.

THE SHOES

I had once tried on the Master's shoes
And found them very comfortable.
But soon, realized the shoes were difficult to fill.

Needing the help of the Master, I asked quickly,
And with his loving gaze, I felt deeply reassured
That one day I shall be more and more like him.

Each step now, brings me closer to the Heart of
God, knowing how blessed I am for the Master, as
Soul reminds me daily to put on the Master's
shoes.

THE SOUND

There is a dance in the Sound
      Having heard it before

Now it is sweeter than honey, jam, or any preserve,
      As Soul dances with the melody

           Into the Light beyond…

THE WINDOW OF TIME

There is a viewing window of time;
All your lives, past, present and future,
Are there for you to see when you are ready.

The now can still change your future,
Knowing your past can influence your now,
You may turn your timeline into some patterns.

Known by many as the wheel of karma,
Records are kept on your deeds, past and present,
With balanced karma, you enter heavenly worlds.

And you may never believe any of this,
You may call it someone's over active imagination,
Until a spiritual master says, "Let's take a look".

TO MY BUTTERFLY

My wife is a sweet butterfly,
Maybe, you know someone like her.

She dances in the air while traveling about,
Admiring babies and children of all ages

Spreading kindness and good cheer
While touching the hearts of everyone, and

Making a lasting impression as one who cares;
I too am grateful for what she does.

Knowing her gift is love,
For it's often the little acts of kindness

That count so very much,
And she adds her unique personal touch.

TREASURES

You are the flowers in my heart,
The flowing breeze against my cheeks,
You are my footprint on the sandy shore.

You are the birds singing a love song,
And the mountains standing strong,
You are my brightest shining stars.

You have taught me so very well,
As I weep with a heart of love and joy,
You keep filling my being even more.

TRUE, NECESSARY, AND KIND

Could it be you are out of your mind?
Yes, one would be out of his mind,
Or above it most of the time, to live
By not saying anything unless it is
TRUE, NECESSARY, AND KIND!

Don't we all want to say something that is
Unkind or something that is half true,
Things we know are not necessary to do.
This leads us to some thoughts about
What the Bible calls, "The Golden Rule".

Treating others the way you want
Them to treat you, certainly makes
Sound, solid, and very wise advice;
Biting one's tongue is much better
Than having to pay a karmic price.

VISUALIZING MASTERSHIP

You are enlightenment.
You are the inner light.
You visualize the Master.

You see with his eyes.
You hear with his ears.
You speak with his tongue.

Become one with his vision.
Become one with his heart.
Become one with his humility.

Be the Light and Sound.
Be the truth you seek.
Be the servant to Spirit.

Know you are Divine.
Know you are one with all.
Know you belong with God.

WORDS FROM A STRANGER

You and I are not so different.
We want to love and to be loved.
We want our life to count for something.
We want at least a measure of understanding.

You and I are not so different.
We sometimes feel alone in a crowd.
We sometimes feel trapped in depressive moods.
We sometimes feel the effects of negative thinking.

You and I are not so different.
We wish for things we do not have.
We wish not to have some things we do have.
We wish, yet take for granted, our greatest gifts.

You and I are not so different.
We can make a difference, we always can.
We can change the world with one more smile.
We can even find and define our true life purpose.

YOU ARE SOUL

You are the light of God's love.
You are the sound of God's heart.
You are the joy in God's divine smile.

You are loved unconditionally.
You are the key to spiritual awareness.
You are the doorkeeper of your own truth.

You are expanding consciousness.
You are the creator of your world.
You are the child of God's Soul.

YOU ARE

You are a cosmic vessel of God's Ocean of Divine
Grace, with a revelation that the distance between
Here and there is only separated by Soul's breath.

Within that breath, you are now on the sands of the
Gobi desert. As you observe the crystal clear night
Sky, you begin counting your blessings, as if
Counting the radiant stars of God.

You realize as infinite as the stars and the grains of the
desert sand, blessings flow as Divine Grace keeps
expanding to the fringe of eternity.

As the mind is trying to comprehend, your true self
Has limitless ability and may now be in the joyous
Center of God's blissfulness.

FOURTH OF JULY

My lover and me,
We sat on a blanket
In view of the distant trees.

My eyes could not
Leave the shades of
Green, her beautiful eyes displayed.

As we nibbled on
A delightful picnic feast,
She had my full attention.

Amongst family and friends
I saw no one
Except my lover there.

We sat on the bank
Of the Potomac
When the fireworks came.

They were anticlimactic,
Magnificent in every respect, but no match
For the sparkles bursting within our hearts.

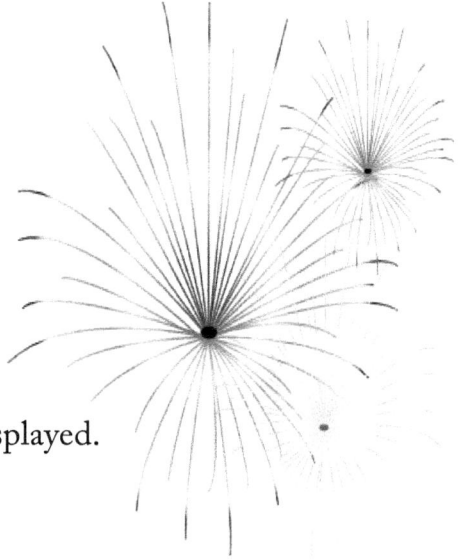

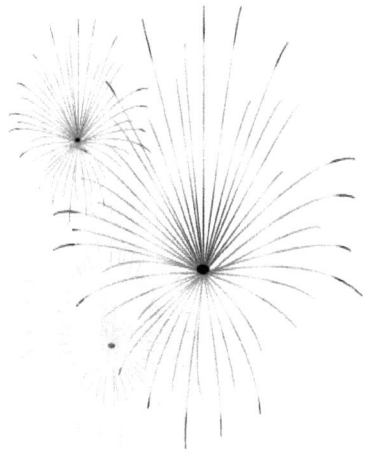

HOW FAST WE ASK

When a problem presents its' self,
We ask the problem be removed,
Before we have seen the lesson in it.

If it is taken away from us,
Something like it may only reappear,
Until we learn what is there behind it.

It may be there to teach us not to fear,
Or to refocus our attention to what matters,
Or to learn to be more patient and tolerant.

Whatever, it may be don't deny it,
Look at it from a spiritual view and with
Gratitude, as another rung on your ladder.

AFFIRMATIONS

I AM A GIFT OF DIVINE LOVE
I AM A VESSEL FOR SPIRIT
I AM A VESSEL FOR GOD

EACH DAY I OPEN MY HEART
TO BE OF SERVICE TO ALL
THE HU SONG STAYS ON MY TONGUE

I LISTEN TO THE INNER VOICE
AND FOLLOW ITS' LEAD
AND CHALLENGES SIMPLY DISSOLVE

I OVERFLOW WITH GRATITUDE
WHILE COUNTING BLESSINGS AS
MY HEART GIVES AND RECEIVES
LOVE PURE

AND, I DWELL IN HUMBLENESS,
WITHIN THE FOUNTAIN OF ALL CREATION, AS I AM

Lem's

FAVORITE
QUOTES ...

"I don't know what your destiny will be, but I do know one thing: the only ones among you will be happy are those who have sought and found how to serve."

— Albert Schweitzer

"Love is patient and kind; love does not envy or boast; it is not arrogant or rude. It does not insist on its own way; it is not irritable or resentful; it does not rejoice at wrongdoing, but rejoices with the truth. Love bears all things, believes all things, hopes all things, endures all things. Love never ends. As for prophecies, they will pass away; as for tongues, they will cease; as for knowledge, it will pass away."

1 Corinthians 13; 4-8

"Be thankful for what you have; you'll end up having more. If you concentrate on what you don't have, you will never, ever have enough."

— Oprah Winfrey

"I am grateful for all of my problems. After each one was overcome, I became stronger and more able to meet those that were still to come. I grew in all my difficulties."

— James Cash Penney

"If I have the belief that I can do it, I shall surely acquire the capacity to do it even if I may not have it at the beginning."

— Gandhi

Soul yearns to leave the limits of time and space that encompass the events of the Earth; to leave behind the karma which binds us here, to gain liberation of Soul, to gain the attributes of God: wisdom, power, and freedom."

— Harold Klemp

"When you do things from your soul, you feel a river moving in you, a joy."

— Rumi

"Life is ten percent what you make it and 90 percent how you take it."

— Unknown

"Love has nothing to do with what you are expecting to get — only what you are expecting to give — which is everything. What you will receive in return varies. But it really has no connection with what you give. You give love because you love and cannot help giving. It is your nature, it is what you do."

— Katherine Hepburn

"Happiness is not in our circumstances but in ourselves. It is not something we see, like a rainbow, or feel, like the heat of a fire. Happiness is something we are."

— John B. Shesin

"Live with intention. Walk to the edge. Listen hard. Practice wellness. Play with abandon. Laugh. Choose with no regret. Appreciate your friends. Continue to learn. Do what you love. Live as if this is all there is."

— Mary Anne Radmacher

"Most people, sometime in their lives, stumble across truth. Most jump up, brush themselves off, and hurry on about their business as if nothing has happened."

— Sir Winston Churchill

"Beloved, let us love one another: for love is of God; and everyone that loveth is born of God, and knoweth God. He that loveth not, knoweth not God; for God is love."

1 John 4:7-8

"Don't wait for something big to occur. Start where you are, with what you have, and that will always lead you into something greater."

— Mary Manin Morrissey

"Explore and understand your own state of consciousness. This should help you move forward into other areas of consciousness beyond your own."

— Harold Klemp

"I've kept a little diary of the ways during the day that I have lost it, that I got caught into the drama of it all, that I started to take it as real. I'd just make a list of it and then look at the patterns of those lists over days. They showed me what it was that I made real.

I think that because it's often so subtle in the way it catches us, that unless you really bring mindfulness to it, you don't see the toxicity of the culture you are living in and the way it takes you and narrows you into a certain definition of yourself."

— Ram Dass

"Nothing contributes so much to tranquilize the mind as a steady purpose – a point on which the soul may fix its' intellectual eye."

— Mary Shelley

"The greatest obstacles to inner peace are disturbing emotions such as anger, attachment, fear and suspicion, while love and compassion and a sense of universal responsibility are the sources of peace and happiness."

— Dalai Lama

"Even though there are many miles between us I hope you know that every minute I stand by you and I love you with all of my heart."

— Bette Tryon

"Even though I am unable to be with you now, every time you feel a breeze on your face, I am sending you my love."

—Mary Cummings

"Be yourself: everyone else is already taken."

— Oscar Wilde

ABOUT THE AUTHOR
LEMUEL WHITELOCK

Lemuel (Lem) Whitelock is a Life Coach who teaches his clients contemplation and visualization techniques. He received his professional certification through The Success Coach Institute www.successcoachinstitute.com, and has designed his coaching practice to assist people in their own self-discovery. He says, "All aspects of a client's life can change when they are aligned with their inner awareness."

Lem has had a wide range of professional experience. While in the Air Force he was a Security Police Officer and K-9 Handler. After leaving the military, he returned to college, and at that time, he began helping others to train their pets. Lem has spent many years in retail and outside sales, and business ownership.

More recently, he has been involved with the Shenandoah Area Agency on Aging, where he has taken wheel chair clients to their medical appointments. He is a Blue Ridge Hospice volunteer and a Big Brother.

Lem is a family man; he has been married to his wife Valerie for over 30 years. They have two grown, adopted children, their son, Doug from Guatemala, and their daughter, Julia from Korea. As a cancer survivor, Lem knows the value of having a supportive and compassionate family.

One of Lem's many passions is writing poetry. When he contemplates, he experiences a shift in consciousness, and while in that state, words can flow into poems. He wants his poetry to convey his love for others, his striving for inner awareness, and his endless devotion to our ever present, Divine Creator.

Lemuel Whitelock

Email: awarenesscenter@yahoo.com
or visit him online at
http://awarenesscentercoaching.wordpress.com

CREDITS

Photography, illustrations and pictures are Royalty-Free [RF] and Public Domain [PD]

p 6   White waters rush over rugged stone at Pee Wee Falls at Boundary Dam in northeastern Washington. Jeff Tetrik.

p 12 White SWAN © Gfadel | Dreamstime.com ID: 215198

p 13 Inkwell - Quill-pen-parchment-and-ink-bottle.jpg http://www.fotosearch.com

p 15 WHITE FLOWER © Cristina Bernhardsen | Dreamstime.com ID: 113790

p 17 Candle [RF] http://www.fotosearch.com [RF] [PD]

p 19 Cattle 1210010160Q97Q [RF] http://www.fotosearch.com

p 21 Old Man http://www.fotosearch.com [RF] [PD]

p 23 CEMETERY CROSS © Grinerswife | Dreamstime.com ID: 185549

p 25 RUSHING RIVER © Tyback | Dreamstime.com ID: 193893

p 27 SUNSET © Ron Hilton | Dreamstime.com ID: 193167

p 29 Dancing Free Illustration [RF] [PD]

p 31 True-beauty <a href="http://www.publicdomainpictures.net/view-image.php?image=25456&picture=true-beauty">True Beauty...</a> by Bobbi Jones Jones

p 32 Fireworks on the river BOMBS BURSTING IN AIR © Angela Farley | Dreamstime.com

p 33, 76 COUPLE SITTING IN FRONT OF WATERFALL. © James Hearn | Dreamstime.com Horsetail falls in Oregon ID: 39403

p 34 Red Tulip <a href="http://www.publicdomainpictures.net/view-image.php?image=500&picture=tulip">Tulip</a> by Anna Langova

p 35 ASTER © Tolchik | Dreamstime.com ID: 239442

p 37 Contemplation endoftheearth.jpg Horizon Illusion, Matt looks out to sea. [PD] [Public Domain] Dylan O'Donnell 2010

p 38 Clouds http://www.publicdomainpictures.net [RF] [PD]

p 39 Sun Wheat http://www.publicdomainpictures.net [RF] [PD]

p 41 Clouds on water http://www.publicdomainpictures.net [RF] [PD]

p 42, 53 Intertwined Heart by Ashley White http://www.clker.com/clipart-intertwined-heart-4.html

p 43 Hearts Of Love <a href="http://www.publicdomainpictures.net/view-image.php?image=21927&picture=heart-of-love">Heart Of Love</a> by Jiri Hodan

p 45 MOUNTAIN REFLECTION © Nancy Mahnken | Dreamstime.com A northern Ga mountain reflected in lake, ID: 190409

p 47 FIELD OF SUNFLOWERS WITH SKY AND CLOUDS. © Peter Zaharov | Dreamstime.com ID: 1761191

p 49, 79 The Star Sun <a href="http://www.publicdomainpictures.net/view-image.php?image=23444&picture=the-star-sun">The Star Sun</a> by Bobbi Jones Jones

p 51 Step Stone Bridge Charlesdrakew
http://en.wikipedia.org/wiki/File:Harewood_stepping_stones.JPG

p 52 Stormy sea at night, by Ivan Aivazovsky 1849
http://en.wikipedia.org/wiki/File:Stormy_sea_at_night.jpg

p 55 SEAGULL IN FLIGHT © Dana Rothstein | Dreamstime.com ID: 65661

p 57 Candle Light by OCAL http://www.clker.com/clipart-candle-light.html

p 59 Alluring Cascades Pirouette by Forest Wander http://www.forestwander.com/2011/11/alluring-cascades-pirouette/

p 61 Loving Couple by Kristian Sekulic iStock_000009524522XSmall

p 63 Red rose http://www.clker.com

p 64 ROSE © Pakhnyushchyy | Dreamstime.com ID: 2481283

p 65 Red Maple http://www.publicdomainpictures.net [RF] [PD]

p 67 Twinn Falls State Park by Forest Wander http://www.forestwander.com/2012/04/twinn-falls-state-park-wv-marsh-fork-falls/

p 68 Silouetted Kiss by OCAL http://www.clker.com/clipart-silhouetted-kiss.html

p 69 WALKING A PATH © Dennis Sherman | Dreamstime.com ID: 186714

p 71 GATE FOR SOULS © Radu Razvan Gheorghe | Dreamstime.com ID: 85755

p 73 Chalice and ring by OCAL http://www.clker.com/clipart-chalice-and-ring.html

p 75 Shoes, 1888 Vincent van Gogh (Dutch, 1853–1890) photo of oil on canvas

p 76 COUPLE SITTING IN FRONT OF WATERFALL. © James Hearn | Dreamstime.com Horsetail falls in Oregon ID: 39403

p 77 EAGLE OWL © Adrian Jones | Dreamstime.com ID: 93896

p 79 The Star Sun <a href="http://www.publicdomainpictures.net/view-image.php?image=23444&picture=the-star-sun">The Star Sun</a> by Bobbi Jones Jones

p 80 Farmers Heavenly Glory http://www.publicdomainpictures.net [RF] [PD]

p 81 THE WINDOW © Slidepix | Dreamstime.com

p 82 Butterfly http://www.publicdomainpictures.net [RF] [PD]

p 83 WILD SUNFLOWER © Brandon Holmes | Dreamstime.com ID: 185196

p 84 Flying Dove www.clker.com/clipart-29963.html

p 85 Orchid http://www.clker.com [RF] [PD]

p 86 Apple to orange http://www.publicdomainpictures.net [RF] [PD]

p 87 Rainbow Gods Earth Covenant ForestWander Nature Photography http://www.feedreader.com/feed/Free_Nature_Pictures_by_ForestWander_Nature_Photography/16425646

p 88 OCEANVIEW CACTI © Rocky Reston | Dreamstime.com ID: 86625

p 89 Fireworks Illustration http://www.clker.com [RF] [PD]

p 90 Wildflowers Rocks Spring Mountain Trail by Forest Wander http://www.forestwander.com/2010/04/wildflowers-rocks-spring-mountain-trail

p 91 Buddha http://www.publicdomainpictures.net [RF] [PD]

p 92 Bluestone Valley View by Forest Wander http://www.forestwander.com/2012/04/bluestone-valley-view/

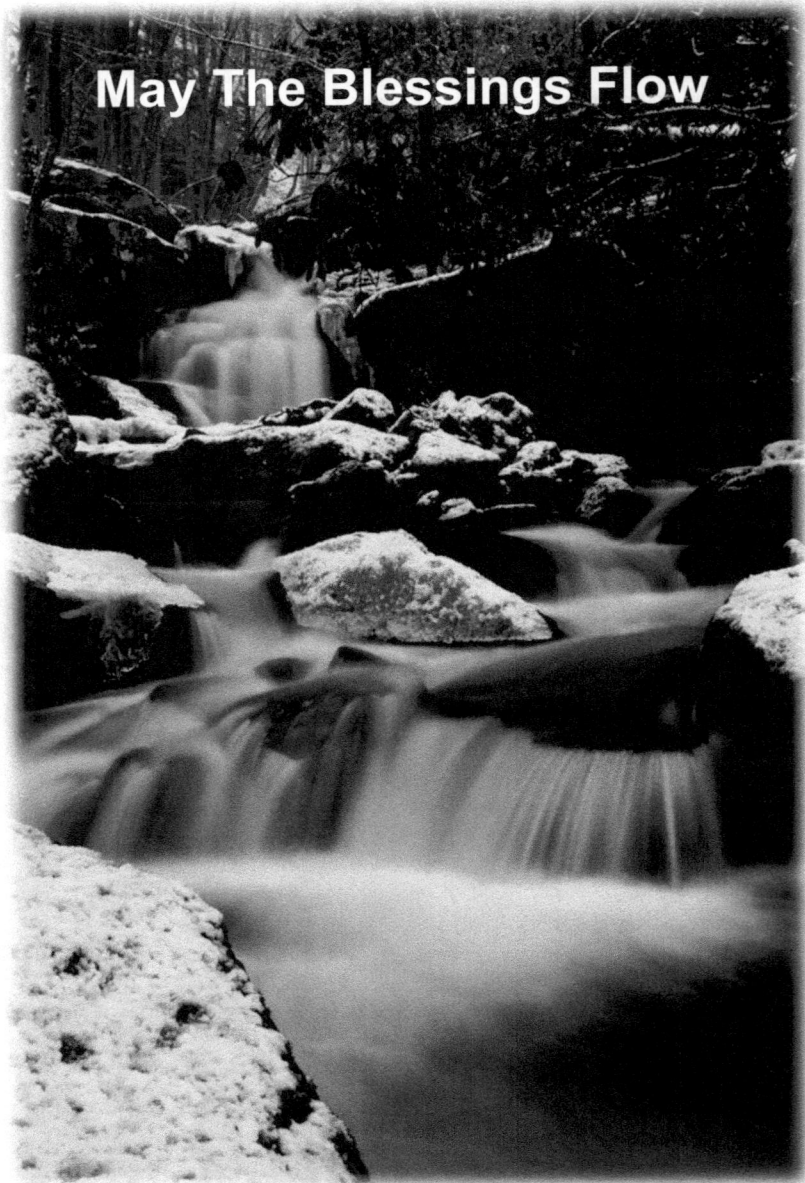

May The Blessings Flow

Winter Waterfall Rocks and Ravine

www.ingramcontent.com/pod-product-compliance
Lightning Source LLC
LaVergne TN
LVHW021539080426
835509LV00019B/2725